The 30 LOVE Laws

Derrick T. Clark

The Gift

Often mistreated battered and overlooked
Then in an instant reappearing to get you hooked
Beautiful, majestic and full of life
Ignorant, unrelated and unsupportive of strife
Single, happy yet quite unaware that
One kiss, one hug, one goodnight
And you're halfway there
Beginning with an infatuation
Continuing with a passion
And persisting with that
That some would only believe to be fate
Realizing the greatest gift of all
Comes from above
How on earth could there be so much hate
Lingering in the distance
To give the unbeliever a lift
Open your heart, your mind, your soul
To witness the world's greatest gift...
The Gift of LOVE!

SINSEAR

The 30 Love Laws

We all have a basic need for acceptance and affection. This basic need is energized from within. From the day we were born, we have to have the affection of another to survive. We receive this by being fed and nurtured in order to grow. Just as we accept milk into our bodies for nourishment, we also accept affection.

The same actions that help us to get taller and stronger help us to first experience what LOVE is. This four letter word is the most rewarding, gratifying, illusive, controversial, and misunderstood words to the human race. We grow more mature and search for the same type of affection that created us. A great number of us find it at one point or another. However, it's questionable how long it will last. The individuals involved answer the question with how they define LOVE.

So, what is LOVE? Many definitions focus on the emotional and physical aspects of this very important word. There are two remaining components that are essential in a romantic relationship. The friendship and spiritual elements add solidarity to the definition. This gives us a foundation for LOVE that is emotional, spiritual and friendship. These elements give us a clear definition.

Most often we focus on the element that has the least longevity. Our emotions lead us to feel a certain way for a particular point in time. That is why your elder would say, "You're experiencing puppy love." They believe this to be the case because of the fresh emotion of a new kind of relationship. What our elders understand is that emotion alone can not sustain LOVE. We make this true also with our differing levels of maturity.

There has to be other elements to sustain that powerful four letter connection. Friendship would be the next element to add for a strong foundation. It's vital, whether it happens in how we meet initially or in the dating process. Having a friend, in your mate, allows for freedom to be who you truly are. Support means the world to us in dealing with daily circumstances. Just imagine a mate that is always willing to accept, support and give you affection. How many marriages would be saved? How many children would grow to see the beauty of the relationship (to make their choices easier)? Even though these elements provide a good foundation, it's not yet complete.

The spiritual aspect provides solidarity and adds a permanent element, like a true friend. Spirituality can mean something different to anyone you ask, like LOVE. This is why it is often the missing link. However, it helps us to gain understanding of the other elements. The focus of spirituality is on the energy inside of us. It is a principle and an awareness that is greater than us all. The self-awareness helps us to understand what is within and what surrounds us. So, how does this apply to LOVE?

Once you have a greater understanding of self, then you understand your magnet. Your magnet attracts everything to you. The attractions will be good and bad but your awareness will decipher. When you recognize that special someone, the spiritual element shall reside between the two. It becomes the bigger principle, acts to strip us of selfish pride and permits us to focus on unification. Often, small things break us apart due to lack of recognition for the bigger picture. These three elements and The 30 Love Laws will aid us in finding and maintaining the thing we all need the most. The most powerful word in any language... LOVE.

The 30 Love Laws

Law 1: Choose Happiness
Law 2: Realize Greater
Law 3: Be Open
Law 4: Don't Be Shallow
Law 5: Understand You
Law 6: You Are The Problem
Law 7: You Are The Solution
Law 8: Affection for Self
Law 9: Know What's Important
Law 10: Affection For Others
Law 11: Learn Your Lessons
Law 12: Have A Passion
Law 13: Believe It's Possible
Law 14: Say What You Need
Law 15: Relationship Reasons

Law 16: Healthy Associations
Law 17: Be What You Want
Law 18: Friendship Foundation
Law 19: Karma Exists
Law 20: Everything Must Fit
Law 21: Don't Settle
Law 22: Mutual Respect
Law 23: Be Consistent
Law 24: Mutual Growth
Law 25: Peacefully Disagree
Law 26: Unify
Law 27: Communicate
Law 28: Truth Always
Law 29: Progress Reports
Law 30: See Big Picture

Law 1: Choose Happiness

Happiness, like everything in life, is a choice. Our surroundings look, feel and attract differently when this choice is made.

We all have a choice with everything in life. This is true even if we are simply making a decision on how we respond to something. For example, we choose where we work with our education levels. We choose our mates, based on what we like. We even choose how our day goes, based on how we start it. Have you ever started a day not wanting to get out of bed? Then, the majority of the day supports why you didn't want to leave bed. It seems as if nothing goes in your favor.

The key is the attitude when we start the day. That is exactly how happiness works. First, we need to understand what makes us happy. It is possible for things or people to make us happy, temporarily. No person or thing can sustain our happiness. The reason for this is, the source is inside of us. What does this mean? Ask yourself a few questions. What are my most positive attributes (outside of the physical)? What matters most (outside of money & things)? What brings me joy? In finding these answers, we can discover our happiness.

We should be happy to know that there is greatness within all of us. This can only be uncovered through focus. It is meant for us to find our happiness and anything or anyone contributes. There will always be outside influences to how we feel. Our foundation should always be rooted in choice. Finding happiness before that special someone comes along is ideal. When we are happy, we attract and recognize others that are as well. The decisions we make say how happy we truly are.

Law 2: Realize Greater

When we realize something greater than us, a culture of selfishness is not possible. This allows for a give/receive culture. We also become aware of the energy that links us all together.

There is a greatness that resides within each and every one of us. When we become aware of this is very important to our lives. Having this awareness, gives us an understanding that there is something more important than oneself to the big picture. This breeds a culture of unselfishness. The idea is to give in order to receive. A great act of kindness is to put someone or something before self. For example, giving time to a worthy cause provides unparalleled fulfillment. The reason for this fulfillment is because we open our spirits to receive through service or giving.

Acts of kindness, from our hearts, sew the right seeds. These seeds will reap a beautiful harvest. Operating on a principle greater than us, keeps us in check for proper perspective. Our spirits are represented by our energy. When we realize the power of this energy, we'll discover what we are truly capable of. That capability will only lack in our ability to imagine. Our imagination is vital in also realizing that there is a special someone made for each of us. The fact that we have the ability to think of someone special makes it possible for them to exist.

Law 3: Be Open

Opening ourselves to unlimited possibilities will allow for great things to be received.

There is a saying that states, "A closed mouth doesn't get fed." This is also a true statement with matters of the heart. You want to allow yourself to be open in order to receive. Life is full of great things that can come in the form of experience. Our experiences, naturally, come from the experience of others until we are able to experience for ourselves. For example, we are taught to like what we are fed, in our youth, until we discover our own likes and dislikes.

We won't always like what we are faced with. This is a part of the process that teaches us how to choose. A new experience, regardless of the outcome, is valuable to us. If we aren't open, it eliminates opportunity and blocks potentially great things. The goal is to have as many possibilities presented to us as we can have. Variations allow us to practice our freedom of choice. That very practice serves us in broadening our outlooks. Many are afraid to give the unknown a fair opportunity. We should always give ourselves a chance to receive something or someone great.

Law 4: Don't Be Shallow

When we only look at the surface, we get surface results. To receive something deeper, we must see and feel below the surface.

From the very beginning, we were taught to believe what we see. What if there is an additional way to determine who or what is in front of you? There is something that we should trust even more than sight. More important than what we see and hear, is what we feel. We are able to connect with others when we connect with what's inside of us. This deeper connection will allow us to get past a calculating surface. If we rely on what we feel, first, we can get the best results.

What we feel should also support what we see and hear. That enables us to discern and keeps us clear of a shallow outlook. There is power that lies beneath. We take away from this power when we make decisions based only on the physical. An example of this is when we choose what looks or sounds best to us. However, we still have a need to feel good. This changes how we see without us noticing. What we feel should clarify the interest in what we see. That is the meaning to the expression, "Love is blind."

Law 5: Understand You

Knowing who and what we are is critical to the choices we make. Every selection says who we are. Awareness is key.

Who would you say you are? Not just your name, but in principle, by the standards that you choose for yourself. What would you say you are? Not just when you look in the mirror, but beneath it all. We must all have answers to these questions to understand ourselves. Establishing principles and discovering who/what we are provide the framework to our own personal greatness.

You can be who you want to be, regardless of the circumstance. All of us have the same general tools. How we use them make the difference. A couple of those tools are value and purpose. Once we discover these things, our next step is to believe through visualization and practice. This will lead others to believe what you do about self. It holds true in our individual greatness and in love.

Awareness is key in every choice we make. It says who/what we are based on our perceived value and purpose. These two are very closely connected in every selection process.

Law 6: You Are The Problem

When things go wrong in our lives, we are to blame. Even when we don't choose, that's still a choice. Recurring problems indicate lack of proper attention.

Many of us blame the wrong source for our issues. The truth is there is one common source for every problem we have. That source for all of our issues is <u>us</u>. We are always the common denominators in our misfortunes. This is a harsh reality for many of us. Why is that so? One of the hardest things that we can do, as human beings, is take a look at ourselves. Here is the question you should ask when problems occur. Was I an active participant in any situation that led to the issue? Without question, this answer will be, yes. We can only "allow" ourselves to be treated in a manner that isn't consistent with our value and purpose.

There are also times when we experience the same issues. This provides evidence that we have not taken the proper time to understand our problem. We are largely capable of basic problem-solving. The key is making the issue a priority. Anyone or anything that is worthy of our time is worth the attention. Reflecting on the problem, outside of emotion will lead to clarity and better choices.

Law 7: You Are The Solution

We have the ability to control everything in our world. This is true in how we react and in our decision-making.

When we own blame, we are on the right path. Understanding the source of any issue can lead to the fix. To attain the fix, we must ask ourselves a couple of questions. Why was a particular decision made? For example, I made a bad dating choice because of loneliness. How was that decision made? For example, I didn't pay attention to glaring signs, initially. The ability to reflect on and answer those questions will change the way a choice is made. An example of this would be to allow yourself to be comfortable alone, without being lonely. This makes you the priority and not the loneliness.

At that point, our standards can take over to aid in our decisions. Now, there is a principle behind our selection process. Exercising our control in the matter, to get the best result, is the goal. Reaction is secondary and resolution breeds success. We must be proactive in every decision-making process.

Law 8: Affection For Self

Having a deep affection for self shows others what to love, beyond what is seen. This type of practice acts against infatuation.

The most important person that you can have affection for is yourself. This is not a vain practice when the topic is love. We must have a deep affection for self before we can properly give to another. Putting the love for self on display allows for others to see how and what to love as well.

Many of us focus on how we look, height, weight, etc. How we feel about all of these things can be changed. To accomplish this, we must look within to ask a couple of questions. How do you feel about the kind of person you are? Do you strive to do good (for yourself and others)? We must be able to answer these questions in a positive way. Our feelings, about self, have a great deal of influence on how we feel about everything. Spend time with yourself and have a great time doing it!

We are all beautifully made and unique. This understanding will become the root for all other affection. The depth of the connection with self allows for other connections of depth.

Law 9: Know What's Important

Understanding what is important is imperative when determining your standards. These standards help to eliminate the unworthy.

What has priority in your life? Are your priorities truly important? How you establish what is important in your life is imperative. We must be able to set standards in order to keep us on track. If this is not done, we can lose sight of what our priorities are. Standards provide structure for us. The structure provides a means to uphold principle.

So, how do we come to an understanding of what is important? We should ask ourselves a simple question. How long will a specific thing matter? For example, family and faith are great things to consider as priorities. These two examples will not fade over time. We must keep in mind that time is the most valuable of things. The time that we are given should be filled with the people and circumstances that are deserving. First, we make sure that we are worthy of time ourselves. Then, knowing what priority people or things hold in your life is clear.

Law 10: Affection For Others

There is fulfillment in exercising affection for another. We all have something to give in order to receive abundantly.

It is important, as human beings, that we have a general affection for others regardless of sex, color, creed or orientation. We have a tendency to focus on how we are different. The beauty of all of us is that there is always something that makes us the same. This should be our focus. It allows us to see ourselves in another. That will be no different in your selection of a mate.

The more you see yourself in your mate, the tighter the bond. We just have to be sure to focus our selection process on the worthy. Opposites only attract due to the intrigue. However, over time your differences will lead you apart. This will certainly be the case if standards are not aligned.

These fundamentals have to be there for mates and friends alike. The best of your circle will be able to grow with or encourage your growth. This distinction must be made for those you choose to have the closest. There is fulfillment in exercising affection. So, we must be selective with our special affection, to give properly and receive abundantly.

Law 11: Learn Your Lessons

Taking time to evaluate what has happened to us in our lives give valuable tools for growth.

When we learn our lessons in life, it enables us to make better choices. Confidence is a key component in always making the best choice. To establish confidence, we must reflect to understand what lesson we should learn.

We select one of two roles when we reflect. Our choice is to be either a victim or a victor. When we choose the victim role, that says, we prefer to point the finger. In situations where we choose the victor role, that says we are able to focus on overcoming. Our attitude helps us to define what role we select, consistently. Victims are likely to experience the same type of issues repeatedly. Victors evaluate circumstances to learn their lessons.

We often make bad choices and justify them as "bad luck" or "tough times." The fact is, what usually happens to us is a result of poor decision-making. This is especially true with the treatment that we allow and mate selection. Once we're able to learn our lessons, we'll have valuable tools for growth.

Law 12: Have A Passion

Having a passion allows us to exercise love regularly. This gives us a means to practice freely.

We all need a way to exercise love. Having a passion allows us to experience fulfillment. Discovering and practicing our passion freely is rewarding without any setbacks. It is quite different from loving someone who may or may not reciprocate. Our passions provide us with a healthy way to give on an emotional level. Exercising this love regularly also opens our hearts and builds stamina. Many of us don't make the correlation. However, the same feelings experienced with a passion are experienced in a great relationship.

The significance is that a passion prepares us for our greatest challenge. That challenge is giving the selfless act of love. A passion will also serve us well inside of the relationship to maintain who we are. This instrument provides joy and, if used inclusively, can encourage a great connection with your mate.

Law 13: Believe It's Possible

Exceptional does not exist without belief. To not believe is to accept normalcy.

How is it possible for us to have anything great if we don't believe in the possibility? The truth is we won't. For anything great to happen to us, on a regular basis, we must believe that it can. This sounds simple but requires devotion. What we believe about ourselves sculpt our world.

Our beliefs show in our language, relations and actions. For instance, those who believe in great possibility speak in certain terms like "when" or "going to." Those who don't believe, use terms like "try" or "maybe." Then, the actions usually support one or the other. Our relationships work the same way.

If we are skeptical of everyone, we will draw skeptical people to us. The strongest focus will always prevail. Average and below average exist in a word absent of great possibility. Exceptional does not exist in a world without belief.

Law 14: Say What You Need

Speak what you need into existence. Write it down, to make it real. Wants have different connotations.

Saying what we need gives us specific things to focus on. Our needs also allow us to create standards that are solid. We must understand that there is a difference between a need and a want. Needs have a specific priority attached to them. A want is a distorted view of what we really need.

When we determine what we need, we have the power to speak it into existence. A good practice would be to write it down to make it plain. This also makes it a real possibility and serves as a reminder to your established standard. The desired qualities give you a "partner grocery list."

Wants should not be overlooked. Once we list everything that is important, our wants take a different shape. However, we must be specific. Focusing on what we need often gives us what we truly want.

Law 15: Relationship Reasons

There is a reason for every relationship we have. Understand the reason.

There is always a reason for every relationship we have in our lives. Normally, we look back for clarity. Here is why there is a saying that, "Hindsight is 20/20." The idea is to have clarity on your relationship in the present. When we acquire this type of clarity, it gives us valuable information. We understand who we should spend our time with.

In our lives, we meet everyone for a particular reason. We must understand that reason. People cross our path for a short time, a longer time or a lifetime. This must not be overlooked. There will also be different kinds of people at every juncture. The key is determining the ones who are meant to stay.

All relationships are important. The companions

we choose say a lot about where we are in life. Fact is, we should be able to grow, be loyal and share happiness with our loved one. This is essential for a permanently strong bond with a friend and/or mate.

Law 16: Healthy Associations

Healthy associations provide an environment for meeting great people. Our earliest good relations were formed from our immediate surroundings.

We all must establish healthy associations in our lives. This is true due to the environment that we need for meeting great people. For example, those who want to have good grades may form a study group. These folks would all have the goal of creating an environment for success.

Many of us have the incorrect idea that every association is a friendship. An associate would be someone who may have some of the same interests or may just be interesting. A friend should have many of the same interests, similar values and is an extension of family. The environment can be critical to this assessment.

Our state, at the time we meet someone, will define our relationship. Are we out doing constructive things during our encounter? Are we out just having a good time? Are we down and out when we meet that associate or friend? These are important questions to ask ourselves. We must see that our time has value and it is better spent with healthy associations.

Law 17: Be What You Want

Having a great personality and character can and will attract the same. Be what you want from others.

There is a saying that states, "Opposites attract." However, there is not a reference to whether or not they stay together. It is understood why we would attract an opposite. In the unknown, there is intrigue. Things that are different to us can make us curious.

The key is for us to become the best version of ourselves and attract the same. If we become comfortable with and love ourselves, others follow. Often, we want a polished product, yet we are tarnished. The focus should be placed on personality and character. This is true for us and the person we want to attract.

Connecting with someone is an organic process. It proves the existence if you have ever witnessed anyone who is kind, loving, sincere and honest. That gives just cause to accept no less. Those who settle are saying they accept that they are less. We are the sole influence for what we attract. The power to attain something or someone great lies within us all.

Law 18: Friendship Foundation

To have a foundation of friendship is paramount. We won't have to question our gain. There is nothing we won't do for a friend.

We should seriously consider only dating those we can establish a friendship with. Many are under the misconception that you don't date a friend. Some will say that you will ruin the friendship. Contrarily, this foundation is needed to withstand the test of time.

Your attraction level will change for someone who is not a good friend to you. Many of the things in a relationship require this. For example, listening, understanding and support are all things a friend provides. There will be defining moments that will demand the aforementioned. These defining moments will happen periodically to test whether a person is meant for you.

We must be able to have fun, laugh with and enjoy our mates. Friends stick by each other. This foundation is key for love to be everlasting. It ties the other two elements together and all great unions require it.

Law 19: Karma Exists

We must recognize that what we give is also what we will receive. This is a reality in all cases, no matter how eventual.

Physically and spiritually we will all reap what we sow. It is impossible to harvest without, first, planting the seed. What is of great importance is the type of seeds we plant. Do we plant seeds that support the best us? If not, we can't expect the best possible results in our lives.

We only <u>deserve</u> what we plant in this world. This is in reference to the personal and professional areas of our lives. We do sometimes receive grace or the benefit of the doubt. However, this is only a loan. Our debt still must be paid in how we give of ourselves. Whether positive or negative, it will spread across all areas of our lives. We will always be returned the fruit of what we put out into the world. It is highly important that our output is the very best we have to give, for the best return. No matter how eventual, karma will work for or against us.

Law 20: Everything Must Fit

It will not be a struggle to fit that special someone into our life. Everything has a way of working out seamlessly.

There is a saying that goes, "We make time for the things we want to make time for." More importantly, that special person is supposed to receive dedicated quality time. This is to determine whether it will be an organic fit. The one that we are to spend our time with will be a great compliment to our world. That does not mean that schedules or situations won't change. It just means that time will not be a chore and will encourage growth.

There is nothing we won't do, if we feel it's worth it. Constant struggle signifies that the chemistry is not organic. Repeated tough times, regular disagreements and inability to compromise speaks to the fit. This is similar to attempting to stuff a round peg into a square hole.

Your moments will either build relationship character or tear it apart. That does not mean that the relationship can't work. This is usually what couples mean when they say, "Relationships are hard work." Contrarily, if you love what you do, you'll never work a day in your life. When everything fits, the relationship will work seamlessly.

Law 21: Don't Settle

Refusing to settle allows the opportunity for something great.

Many will say, "Never say never." Nevertheless, we should <u>never</u> settle. When we settle, it sets the stage for us to accept less. This is a culture we should <u>never</u> subscribe to. Settling is a practice that is dangerous to us all as creatures of habit.

So, how do we know if we are truly settling? First, we must determine our value. An honest assessment of ourselves will lead us in the right direction. Once we assess our value, we can't accept less. Everyone we accept into our lives say how we value ourselves.

Then, there are those who will attempt to shame others with an appropriate standard. This says more about their lack of standard. <u>Never</u> feel guilty about standards set honestly. There are those who say that you will always have to accept something. However, this is not true. We all are supposed to have someone great. Those who show potential do not fall in the category of accepting less. Essentially, there must be a desire to exercise that potential for a great relationship.

Law 22: Mutual Respect

Respect is a must for a formidable mate. It enables us to see an equal.

We must consider everything we know about a person when we choose a mate. This assessment is key when determining if our potential is formidable. It's important to realize that there is value in each perspective. We all have our differences. This is the very thing that makes us all unique. However, the beauty lies in what makes us all the same. If this is a primary focus, we will have a healthy respect for our partner.

What does a healthy respect mean to the relationship? It means that there should be an allowance for our mate to be an individual. The idea that we have our mate's support is comforting. Seeking to understand your partner's individual endeavors show that you care about their interests. A quality relationship will be a reciprocal one. It is vital to see the interests of our mate as important as our own. This is why we must have a mate that we consider an equal.

Law 23: Be Consistent

Consistency shows care and significance. This will be valuable to longevity.

Love has been and will always be an action word. Anything said must be followed in action to exhibit truth. "I Love You" is the best and worst phrase you can say to someone, romantically. How could this be true? After this statement is made, it must be proven time and time again. Continuous action and expression shows love to be the priority.

Complacency is both dangerous and natural. This is the first attack on romance which affects how we feel or the emotional element. For example, dating often declines drastically or ceases in relationships over time. This can not happen! There is no excuse, not even kids.

The relationship that produces kids must also show them how to thrive in it. They need you more than ever in this regard. A couple must make each other a priority. The fruit of our relationship is not only in the production of kids. It also lies in how consistent we are with showing each other significance. This will be valuable to longevity.

Law 24: Mutual Growth

Growing together provides an additional bond. The more things accomplished together, the harder it is to drift apart.

Anything that doesn't grow dies! Our relationship is not an exception to this rule. Two people growing in the same direction create an additional bond. The team concept is something that is very important to us. This is why we must be careful with our inner circles, on all levels.

Everyone either contributes to the team concept or takes away. Our mate is the person we encounter the most. So, we have to be in support of one concept. There is a sense of accomplishment in a relationship when things are done as a team. We should have individual and couple goals. The involvement and support in individual goals aid in the pride of accomplishing couple goals. When these things happen, it will be almost impossible to drift apart.

Law 25: Peacefully Disagree

To disagree is healthy and honest. To do this in peace is vital.

The vast differences that exist between us will lead to disagreement. This is expected but is meant to be done in peace. Our differences are merely a celebration of uniqueness. The fact is that we are more alike than different, as people.

Disagreeing is not a bad thing. It gives us an opportunity to communicate and expand our knowledge of each other. Peaceful disagreement is a must in a fruitful relationship. For this to occur, we have to be able to speak outside of the height of emotion. How we disagree means everything. It doesn't mean that we should always agree with our mate. However, we should be able to agree to disagree without holding onto the issue.

Many of us will hold tight to what we feel is right or wrong. Contrarily, it is about exhibiting respect for your mate's position. Our mate only cares whether their feelings matter. The act of peace encourages communication and sets the stage for compromise.

Law 26: Unify

Inside of a committed relationship there is one identity. This doesn't mean that we aren't still individuals. As one is gained, you don't lose the other.

There can only be one identity, as a couple. That identity is based on the sum of who we are individually. An equivalent would be a team focused on defense. Our purpose in a union is to come together to create a solid unit. This unit will shine a light that will affect everyone around you.

We must not lose sight, of the fact, that we are still individuals. It is imperative that we continue to grow, as people, to properly contribute to the union. Two solid individuals make the greatest unit.

Often, we hear folks say that they lost themselves in a relationship. This causes the very fibers of what brought you together to be torn apart. With individuality, our mate must still be included for support and synergy. It is highly unlikely to be fulfilled living for someone else. True fulfillment occurs when we exercise our potential as individuals to maximize the unit.

Law 27: Communicate

We must discuss everything with our mates. This will be the cornerstone of trust.

Nothing can be assumed in a relationship. We have a range of feelings and emotions that must be explored. This is the reason why everything must be discussed. Communicating should not be seen as a negative. It simply means that we should talk regularly.

We are special, as human beings, for our ability to communicate. Many times, it's not done often or properly. To get the things we want, we must be vocal. The only way that this can happen is by being clear, outside of anger.

There are four dreaded words in any relationship, "We need to talk." It also signifies that regular communication is not taking place. Consistent conversation doesn't ever allow for there to be a "need to talk." Our constant conversation serves as a cornerstone of trust. It also helps to keep us closely involved with one another in often busy lives. Communication is the most important aspect of the connection.

Law 28: Truth Always

Honesty is not negotiable. It shows how much we really care.

One thing that must be a top priority, in a relationship, is honesty. We must keep in mind that trust is a cornerstone in building an everlasting unity. Truth does not hurt as much as a lie from someone that you share intimate moments with. In truth, there is nothing to question. How we tell the truth is key. You may have heard the saying, "It's not what you say but how you say it." However, it is essential that we are honest with ourselves first. It will make it easier to be honest with another.

How we share the truth should always be done in a way that is consistent with love. Our word, to those we care the most about, holds value. That value will either be high or low based on our consistency. Lies break the foundation and cause harm to anything that is meant to last forever. The truth in our word, measured with our actions, display how we really love someone.

Law 29: Progress Reports

For every educational process, there is a performance report. This should also be true for our relationship.

The educational process has different ways of tracking our level of success. We need this information to understand our progress or lack thereof. For anything important, we must know how we're doing. It allows us to set clear goals and achieve them.

Progress lets us know that we are moving in a forward direction. In a fruitful relationship, we should give one another constant feedback. Monthly communication, on your progress, would be an example of a good frequency. Making this a regular priority will remove that awkward feeling of having "the talk." We also must be detailed in our assessments.

The key is not to point the finger or focus on the negative. Focusing on what should happen (that's equally beneficial) versus complaining about what isn't happening, makes us all more receptive. This has to done outside of frustration to get the best result. Covering where you are and where you would like to go is the purpose for a relationship progress report.

Law 30: See Big Picture

Small things lose priority to those who only see the big picture.

Why do we commit? The answer to that simple question escapes many. However, the explanation is as simple as the question itself. We all want and need love to be fulfilled. That is just how we are designed.

Once we reach a certain level of maturity, we want the idea of an endless love. We want to know that the person that we are crazy about is as equally or more crazy about us. Though our execution is poor in getting it, committing to the execution (as a team) can change this.

Language would be a great example of a tool to use for a tight union. "I" or "You" does not reflect togetherness. "We" or "Our" would be a way to properly address the unity. This puts LOVE above each of you in the relationship. Isn't this why we commit anyway?

Small things become big without addressing them. We address things with the language we practice towards one another, followed by action. The big picture in any commitment is the love. To say that we are no longer in love, is saying that we have lost sight of the big picture.

The 30 Love Laws Questionnaire

These questions will help you and/or your mate get beneath the surface, where <u>love</u> lives.

1. Am I happy?
2. What makes me happy (outside of money & material things)?
3. Am I living the life that I want to live?
4. What do I attract into my life?
5. What type of people are in my circle (positive or negative)?
6. Are the right things important?
7. Am I the best version of myself right now?
8. Would I commit to me forever?
9. Have I found my passion (which is connected to my gift that contributes to purpose in life)?
10. Am I honest with myself?

The above questions will allow us to become more

aware of who we truly are. To gain power, in our lives, we must have knowledge of self for proper application. There is no power greater than LOVE...

Knowledge + Application = Power

About the Author

Derrick T. Clark also known as SINSEAR (Sincere) is an American born poet/spoken word artist. During his travels abroad, he gained the perspective that people are more alike than different. Ultimately, seeing we all want the same thing. The experience of serving his country and the voiceless allowed him to compile valuable information. This information spans 15 years from the diverse, young and seasoned. His purpose is to help others and himself with the one thing we all want and need more than anything in this world. It's a four letter word called LOVE.

Made in the USA
Columbia, SC
31 October 2024